Citizens' Movements

by Jill Kushner

PEARSON
Scott
Foresman

Editorial Offices: Glenview, Illinois • Parsippany, New Jersey • New York, New York
Sales Offices: Needham, Massachusetts • Duluth, Georgia • Glenview, Illinois
Coppell, Texas • Ontario, California • Mesa, Arizona

ISBN: 0-328-13656-5

4 5 6 7 8 9 10 V0G1 14 13 12 11 10 09 08 07 06

Introduction

In a way, every political action we take in the United States is part of a citizens' movement. We are citizens who make decisions about how our country works.

Sometimes people feel that they need to do more. Being part of a citizens' movement shows personal responsibility. People have to be aware of a problem, and then they need to organize themselves and others. The rest of their work involves education and action. When a citizens' movement is successful, there are positive results.

The idea of citizens' movements is not new in the United States. Our founding fathers were involved in an important citizens' movement when they created our nation.

As colonists settled in North America, they knew they had to be responsible for their future. The English king was an **obstacle** to their independence. The colonists started a citizens' movement that resulted in the American Revolution.

The founding fathers made laws to protect citizens of the newly formed United States of America.

The action taken by citizens to achieve their goals can vary. People might use speeches, gatherings, marches, sit-ins, or boycotts—the refusal to purchase a product—to achieve their goals.

Most citizens' movements have some things in common. They are often the brainchild of a group of people who see something they wish to change and who take responsibility for trying to make that change happen. This is the case with two important citizens' movements: the women's suffrage movement and the movement for Native American rights.

Women's Suffrage
Background

The women's suffrage movement, or the effort of women to win the right to vote, was part of a broader effort aimed at getting equal rights for women. Today, women across the United States still struggle to get equal pay in the workplace, respect for the work they do as homemakers, and **access** to more political power.

The women's rights movement that exists today is a continuation of the struggle women started long ago. They have fought for many years to become equal partners in the political process.

As early as the American Revolution, women were active alongside men in expressing their dissatisfaction with their English rulers. As homemakers, women boycotted English tea. They also spun their own thread so they would not have to use English fabric.

Despite their contributions to the establishment of a new nation, women were not included in early discussions about voting rights. Although Abigail Adams, wife of the second President, encouraged her husband and other political figures to "Remember the Ladies" when they made decisions about the future of the nation, by the 1780s only white male property owners could vote.

Abigail Adams, wife of President John Adams

Women Take Action

In the early 1800s, educational opportunities began to open up for women. They became involved in reform movements, or movements for change. They spoke out against slavery.

Many of the people who fought against slavery before and during the Civil War became supporters of women's suffrage. While enslaved people had been denied rights, women, too, had fewer rights compared with men. They could not own property, and their husbands had all of the **authority** in their homes. Women's responsibilities were only supposed to include the care of their homes and children.

At the World Anti-Slavery Convention in 1840, two women—Lucretia Mott and Elizabeth Cady Stanton—were forced to sit in the galleries instead of in the main hall because they were women. This event, along with the growing need for equality, led to the Women's Rights Convention, which was held in Seneca Falls, New York, in 1848.

Elizabeth Cady Stanton

Lucretia Mott

7

At the Women's Rights Convention, the Declaration of Sentiments was drafted. It called for women to have equal rights in education, property ownership, and citizenship. It used the Declaration of Independence as its model. The Declaration of Sentiments included a section about the need for women to be able to vote. Before reaching this agreement, members of the convention debated for a long time.

After the Civil War ended, the 15th Amendment to the Constitution gave African American males the right to vote. Although they were often prevented from exercising this right, the passage of the 15th Amendment was an important step forward. Meanwhile, women were left behind.

In 1866, Elizabeth Cady Stanton formed the Equal Rights Association to fight for women's suffrage, or right to vote. In 1890, along with Susan B. Anthony, Lucy Stone, and Julia Ward Howe, Stanton formed the National American Woman Suffrage Association. They were joined in their fight by the Woman's Christian Temperance Union, an organization that fought against the drinking of alcoholic beverages.

 The 15th Amendment to the Constitution gave African American men the right to vote.

In 1872, Susan B. Anthony took action when she tried to vote for Ulysses S. Grant in the Presidential election. She was arrested. In 1878, a women's suffrage amendment was introduced.

People who were against women's suffrage argued that women were less intelligent than men. They also argued that men could and should represent their wives. Some people were concerned that women's suffrage and equality might make women neglect their duties as homemakers. But women who were fighting for their rights did not **wilt.**

 Susan B. Anthony was arrested for trying to vote in the Presidential election of 1872.

Women's Rights Time Line

1792: Mary Wollstonecraft calls for the equality of women in her book *A Vindication of the Rights of Women.*

1821: The Troy Female Seminary is founded. It is the first program to offer college-level classes to women.

1848: The first women's rights convention is held in Seneca Falls, New York.

1868: Susan B. Anthony and Elizabeth Cady Stanton begin publishing a women's rights newspaper titled *The Revolution.*

1872: Susan B. Anthony is arrested for voting.

1884: Belva Lockwood runs for President.

1890: The National American Women's Suffrage Association is formed.

1905: At age 85, Susan B. Anthony meets with President Theodore Roosevelt to discuss a suffrage amendment.

1913: A women's suffrage march is held in Washington, D.C.

1920: The 19th Amendment becomes law. Women gain the right to vote. Vice-President Marshall signs the Suffrage Resolution.

Getting Results

The constant efforts of women were finally rewarded in 1920. The 19th Amendment to the Constitution was passed, stating that voting rights could not be denied "on account of sex."

After women won the right to vote, the National American Woman Suffrage Association broke up. Then the League of Women Voters, an organization that still encourages all people to vote and to learn about candidates, was formed. This group is highly respected. It is considered a definitive resource on voting rights for people in all states.

Out of the women's suffrage movement also grew the effort to pass the Equal Rights Amendment, which was first proposed in 1923. In 1961, President John F. Kennedy launched the President's Commission on the Status of Women. Former First Lady Eleanor Roosevelt was the chairperson. The commission found that although American women had voting rights and more educational and financial opportunities than they once had, they still faced inequality when compared with men.

The commission suggested changes to hiring practices that would offer women more career opportunities. They also called for reasonably priced child care and paid maternity leave.

In the next decade, laws were passed to improve the rights of women. One law required that employers pay women the same wages as men if they did the same job. Another said that employers could not discriminate based on gender.

Then in 1972, Congress passed the Equal Rights Amendment. This amendment to the U.S. Constitution said that equal rights under the law of the United States could not be denied or reduced on the basis of gender. This meant women and men would be entirely equal under the law. The amendment never became part of our constitution, however. Not enough state legislatures ratified, or approved, the amendment. It died in 1982.

There is also now a group called the National Organization for Women. This group was formed in the 1960s and continues to publish a national magazine. It acts as a powerful voice for women's rights.

The Equal Rights Amendment, or the ERA, was approved in 35 states. It needed the votes of three more states to become law.

Native American Rights
Background

The rights of Native Americans have been denied for hundreds of years. When early explorers claimed land in America, the people who lived there first were taken advantage of.

How were settlers able to claim the **lush** land that Native Americans had inhabited for centuries? In some cases, the government made treaties with Native American groups, promising control of one area of land in exchange for the land the settlers or the government desired. All too often, though, these treaties were broken when settlers or the government decided they wanted the land that had been given to Native Americans as well. Sometimes settlers or government agents purchased the land outright. Other times, settlers simply moved onto the land and pushed the Native Americans off of it. This method often led to open warfare.

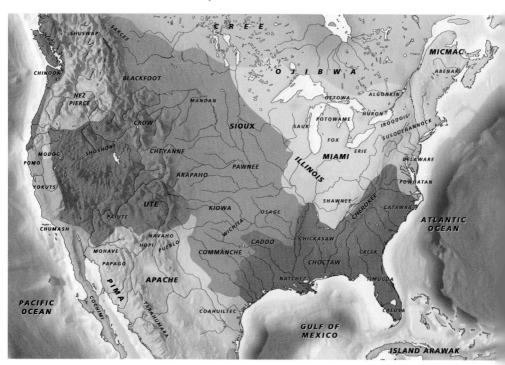

This map shows areas where Native American groups lived prior to the arrival of Europeans.

As the United States grew, hard battles were fought between Native Americans and settlers. In many cases, the U.S. Army stepped in to protect the settlers' interests. The government also created treaties, or agreements, with Native Americans that were supposed to allow them to live on their lands and govern themselves.

The agreements made between Native Americans and the U.S. government were not always upheld. Lands that Native Americans were supposed to keep were taken away from them.

The 1800s were a time when Native Americans were treated with great disrespect. They were removed from their lands and forced to go to other areas where the government wanted them to go. This treatment took its **toll** on them.

In 1830, Congress passed the Indian Removal Act, which was signed into law by President Andrew Jackson. It required many Native American peoples to give up their lands and move to federally designated lands in the West. Often these were poor lands that no white settlers wanted to settle. Some Native Americans submitted to the law while others did not.

In 1838, nearly 20,000 Cherokee people still remained in the East. The government called for them to be forcibly removed. They were sent off on an 800-mile journey, mostly by foot, to what is now Oklahoma. More than a quarter of them died from cold and disease along the way. This journey became known as the Trail of Tears.

As Native Americans were resettled on reservations, they became isolated from one another. They had a hard time surviving in their new settings—often with little help and few resources.

In the late 1800s and early 1900s, the U.S. government began a policy that encouraged Native Americans to assimilate—to become part of the entire American nation—without regard for their rights or needs. Often Native American children were forced to attend schools where they were not permitted to speak their own language or study their own traditions. Sometimes they were even taken away from their parents.

Then laws were passed to force Native Americans to assimilate. Some of these laws were later challenged in the U.S. Supreme Court.

Today, the struggle continues. Native Americans have made significant progress in getting the U.S. government to respect their need to determine their own future. They are still fighting to gain rights to land, water, and sources for food.

 Native American students were forced to assimilate.

Native Americans Take Action

Several groups have been formed on behalf of the tribal rights of Native Americans. One of them, the American Indian Movement (AIM), was created in 1968. In 1972, AIM members took over the Federal Bureau of Indian Affairs in Washington, D.C., for a short time to protest the government's control over Native American affairs.

In 1973, AIM and its followers took over Wounded Knee, South Dakota, a place of **torment** where the U.S. military killed many Native Americans in 1890. In doing this, AIM was attempting to force the government to review more than 300 treaties.

AIM leader and U.S. official make an agreement to end the trouble at Wounded Knee, 1973.

AIM also takes other kinds of action to work for the benefit of Native Americans. In addition to its main mission, which is to make sure that treaties between the government and Native Americans are honored, it has asked for its leaders to address Congress; it has asked for relief money from the government; and it has requested a higher level of respect for Native American culture.

AIM has also worked directly with its members to improve their lives. It staffs and runs a legal center, and schools have been set up for both adults and children to improve their skills. In addition, job training exists for teenagers and adults. As part of its ongoing program of awareness, AIM holds activities to honor historical events that are important to Native Americans.

Traditional powwows are still held today.

Some Progress Is Made

As a result of the organized action of Native Americans, steps are being taken to correct the gross injustices of the past. More conversations are taking place between representatives of Native American groups and the U.S. government.

There is still much to do, but greater attention is being paid to obeying the treaties that were agreed to long ago. In 1996, President Bill Clinton signed a document saying that federal groups must allow Native Americans to have complete control of their lands.

In addition, education about Native American history is taking place. In 2004, the Smithsonian's National Museum of the American Indian (NMAI) celebrated its opening in Washington, D.C. There are also NMAI buildings in New York City and outside of Washington, D.C., in Suitland, Maryland.

 Former President Bill Clinton honors Native American Sacagawea for her key contributions to the Lewis and Clark expedition. The award is accepted on behalf of the Lehmi Shoshone tribe.

The International Indian Treaty Council works for all indigenous, or native, people of the world. In 1994, the United Nations drafted a Declaration of the Rights of Indigenous Peoples. In 2004, protesters staged a hunger strike at the United Nations to express their disappointment that so little progress had been made since the Declaration was first created.

Summary

We have looked at two important citizens' movements—movements for the rights of women and Native Americans—but there are many others. Groups of concerned citizens work on many issues: the rights of people with disabilities, the environment, the protection and safety of children, energy, nuclear weapons, the needs of military personnel and veterans, world hunger, healthcare, senior citizens' care, the arts, and others. Citizens' movements have the power to make a huge impact. They are made up of people who have a strong sense of responsibility and want to make their world a better place.

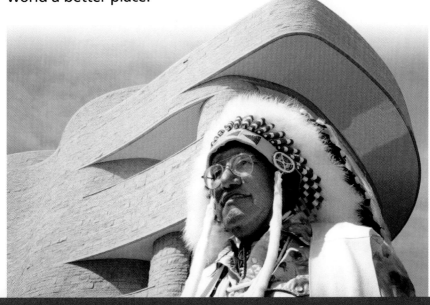

Native groups from North, South, and Central America are featured in the exhibits of the Smithsonian's National Museum of the American Indian.

Glossary

access *n.* a way for means of entrance.

authority *n.* the power to make decisions.

lush *adj.* having much growth, usually plant growth.

obstacle *n.* something that stands in the way of a goal.

toll *n.* something paid, lost, or suffered.

torment *n.* the cause of great pain.

wilt *v.* to weaken or show fatigue.